COMING & GOING

Poems © the authors or their estates, 2019
Illustration and cover image © Gillian Rose, 2019
Edited by Helena Nelson
ISBN 978-1-910131-47-3
All rights reserved

All poems in this anthology have been drawn from
HappenStance pamphlets or books printed between
2005 and 2019. Thank you to all the poets and/or
their families for permission to include them here.
Thanks to Marcia Menter for checking proofs.

NOTE FOR VISUALLY IMPAIRED READERS:

The front jacket of this book white card, textured to create a dimpled effect. The title is centred about two and a half inches from the top in dark brown caps with the word 'and' as an ampersand. The subtitle, Poems for Journeys, is centred below this in black lowercase italics. Below this a dark brown line. In the lower half of the jacket there are 6 small, hand-drawn (in black) images, namely a plane, a ship, a girl on horseback, a car, a man with a dog, and small train. (Inside the book, one of these images appears on the heading page for each section: By Water, By Road, By Horse, On Foot, By Air, and By Rail.) Centred at the bottom of the front jacket is the imprint title in small dark brown caps. The back jacket has a text description of the collection in black at the top. Below this, there is a sample poem (Small Towns') centrally positioned. A barcode appears in black at the foot, together with details of price, press name and logo (small black sphinx).

First published in 2019 by HappenStance Press
21 Hatton Green, Glenrothes KY7 4SD
www.happenstancepress.com

Printed and bound by Imprint Digital, Exeter
https://digital.imprint.co.uk

COMING & GOING

Poems for reading on the train
or tram or bus or aeroplane
or barge. Or hovercraft. Or boat.
Poems to help you stay afloat.

HAPPENSTANCE

CONTENTS

BY WATER

Robbie Burton : 'Some things won't be said goodbye to' /11
Rose Cook: 'Casting Off' / 12
Richie McCaffery: 'Dedication' / 13
Michael Loveday: 'Desert Island' / 14
Helen Clare: 'Gerris Lacustris (Pond Skater)' / 16
Rosemary Hector: 'Bananas' / 17
Laurna Robertson: 'Kiss' / 18
James Wood: 'The Pool' / 19
Tom Cleary: 'On Bassenthwaite, through Binoculars' / 20
Stephanie Green: 'A Visitation' / 21
Martin Edwards: 'Whales' / 22
Niall Campbell: 'North Atlantic Drift' / 23
Tom Vaughan: 'Carthage' / 24
Martin Parker: 'The Shark and the Vest' / 25
Andrew Sclater: 'The Search for My Late Father in Mid-Ocean' /26
Anne Caldwell: 'After the Flood' / 27
M. R. Peacocke: 'Eastham Street' / 28
J. O. Morgan: from 'In Casting Off' / 29
David Ford: 'Evensong' / 30
D. A. Prince: 'Undoing Time' / 31
Kristian Evans: 'Departure' /32

BY ROAD

Lorna Dowell: 'In Case' / 35
Patricia Ace: 'Bull' / 36
Janet Loverseed: 'Je m'ennuie' / 37
Lydia Fulleylove: 'Night Drive' / 38
Matthew Stewart: 'Dad on the M25 After Midnight' / 39
Sue Butler: 'Hunger' / 40
Gill Andrews: 'Tom Potter' / 41
Theresa Muñoz: 'Performance Review' / 42
Alison Prince: 'Early Bus' / 43
Lois Williams: 'Formation' / 44
Margaret Christie: 'Modulation' / 45

C. J. Driver: 'Illegal Immigrants' / 46
Marion Tracy: from *Giant in the Doorway* / 47
Kate Scott: 'Some Afternoons' / 48
Michael Munro: 'Trajectories, Mull' / 49
Martin Reed: 'Right Turn' / 50
Cliff Forshaw: 'Road Kill' / 51
Charlotte Gann: 'Collected' / 52
Rosie Miles: 'When I am dead, my dearest' / 53
Stephen Payne: 'Journey Home' / 54

BY HORSE

Michael Mackmin: 'The Kiss' / 57
Graham Austin: 'Afterthought' / 58
Ruth Marden: 'Little Jockey' / 59
Maria Taylor: 'The Horse' / 60
Jon Stone: 'The New Doctor Who' / 62
Chrissy Williams: 'Robot Unicorn Attack' / 63
Richard Osmond: 'If my instructions have been carried out' / 64
Frank Wood: 'Words to Eat' / 65
Helen Tookey: 'Prairie' / 66
Jim Carruth: 'Rider at the Crossing' / 68
Alison Brackenbury: 'Laminitis' / 69
Jo Field: 'Waterloo' / 70

ON FOOT

Deborah Trayhurn: 'Before we could fly, before' / 73
Ross Kightly: 'Landscapes' / 74
Matt Merritt: 'Cure' / 75
Frances Corkey Thompson: 'The Old Woman Wishes for a Road' / 77
Jeremy Page: 'Snow' / 78
Ruth Pitter: 'The Lost Tribe' / 79
Annie Fisher: 'Sack Race' / 80
Kate Hendry: 'My Father Carries His Death To Me' / 81
Tom Duddy: 'Small Towns' / 82

Gill McEvoy: 'Field of Buttercups' / 83
Andrew Philip: 'Man With a Dove on His Head' / 84
Kirsten Irving: 'Nancy Archer Steps Out' / 85
Patrick Yarker: 'Shoes' / 86
Peter Jarvis: 'Takkies' / 87
David Kinloch: 'Cain's Wife' / 88
Alan Hill: from 'Gerontion' / 89
Lydia Kennaway: 'Walking for Water' / 90

BY AIR

Paula Jennings: 'Swan' / 93
Hamish Whyte: 'First and Last Swan' / 94
Tim Love: 'Iron Birds' / 95
Gerry Cambridge: 'The Queen' / 96
Fiona Moore: 'Night Letter' / 98
Helen Evans: 'Today's Task' / 99
Alan Buckley: 'Gravity' / 100
D. A. Prince: 'Blackbird' / 101
Will Harris: 'Mother's Country' / 102
Gina Wilson: 'Avian' / 103
Clare Best: 'Airman' / 104
Robin Vaughan-Williams: 'The Manager & I' / 105
Martin Cook: 'Falling' / 106
Sally Festing: 'Saturday Morning' / 107
David Hale: 'Deadman Point' / 108
Diana Gittins: from 'Bork!' / 109
Geoff Lander: 'The Diabetes Legacy' / 110
Helen Nicholson: 'Softening' / 112

BY RAIL

Rob A. Mackenzie: 'Girl Playing Sudoku on the 7:14' / 115
Olive Dehn: 'On a Clear Night' / 116
Gregory Leadbetter: 'Persephone on the Underground' / 117
Marilyn Ricci: 'This is a Passing Train that Will Not Stop' / 118

Charlotte Gann: 'Corners' / 119
Christina Dunhill: 'Lost' / 120
Vishvāntarā: 'To Platforms' / 121
Eleanor Livingstone: 'Restore Point' / 122
Stephen Payne: 'Imp of the Perverse' / 124
Alan Buckley: 'The Alchemist' / 125
Marcia Menter: 'Strangers on a Train' / 126
Maria Taylor: 'Travelling on the 10:21 with Tom Hardy' / 128
Paul Stephenson: 'Disposal' / 129
Jennifer Copley: 'Leeds City Station, 1918' / 130
Ramona Herdman: 'He Pretends He Doesn't Know the Way
    to the Station' / 131
D. A. Prince: 'The Sunday Night Piano' / 132
Peter Gilmour: 'Old Man' / 133
Jim C Wilson: 'Mr MacCaig Came to Stirling' / 134
Mark Halliday: 'Noon Freight' / 136
Peter Daniels: 'Mr Luczinski Takes a Tram' / 138
Gerry Cambridge: 'From a Stopped Train Near Arbroath' / 139
Helena Nelson: 'Warning' / 140

Acknowledgements / 141
About Happen*Stance* Press / 144

BY WATER

Robbie Burton:

SOME THINGS WON'T BE SAID GOODBYE TO

For instance, boats.
I tried saying goodbye to one of those.
To its burbling propeller and ticking kettle.
To the doily of sunlight patched above our bed.

Goodbye I said, marking danger points
on my mind's eye map. Trunk roads crossing
hump-backed bridges. Marinas squaring up
to the west coast mainline.

But people giving me lifts don't follow my rules.
They take roads past sudden canals where
lovers still chat on narrow boat roofs
and fall asleep later in firelight.

Rose Cook:

CASTING OFF

She should have let him go ages before
he asked her (several times—I heard him)
but she stands thigh deep, her small hands on
the prow of his boat, offering instructions
in a gentle voice, as an air hostess does before
take-off, her own fears chained together
like clauses and carefully wrapped around
as fast as he tries to cast off, until he can
take it no more and shouts to her to let go
and to shut up since he knows more about sailing
than she does and she waits with her arms
at her sides, watching, while the wind takes
her son and his orange sails and carries him out
far on a run, so he cuts through the slate sea
not looking back, but we can just hear his voice:
I know far more about sailing than you do.

Richie McCaffery :

DEDICATION

In an underground copy
of *Lady Chatterley's Lover*
a shaky plum inscription:

To Renee, my sweet—
from France via the Dunkirk
holocaust, 2/4/40, Sid

All that way in a kitbag,
through panzers and snipers.
Bullets hitting the water
like kingfishers.

Michael Loveday :

DESERT ISLAND (ADVICE FROM A MOTHER)

don't forget
your Rough Guide
ear plugs
swimming trunks

how about
your speed goggles
Anusol
sat nav

what about
your flip chart
what about
your purple pen

how about
your father
how about
your twice removeds

what about
the Polish primer
have you got
my lucky snail

don't forget
my drawing
of the photo
of that fresco

what's with all
the world's a page
what about
the fish in that sea

will you keep
the bird-in-the-hand
will you get
the early worm

how about
the real thing
what about
she's worth it

have you got
the can't forget
don't forget
the can't forget

Helen Clare :

GERRIS LACUSTRIS (POND SKATER)

It turns out that the knack my mother had
of seeking out and bouncing smoothed flat stones
off the surface of Lake Bala depends
on water meshing, like a trampoline
returning the fallen to the sky,
or the atmosphere pushing off spacecraft.

Water clings to itself like mercury,
avoiding air, forming drops as it's sloughed
from drenched dogs. Insect legs stretch the water's shell:
they paddle without piercing or wetness.

It's true too that a mosquito's footfall
does not break dreams, as the skin—oblivious
to air—shrugs off the countless touches
of the day. Talk to me now of ripples.

Rosemary Hector:

BANANAS

Below deck, in the great hall
of the aircraft carrier,
the Admiral stood and welcomed
us, his guests, to the ship.
The case for the Navy, he intoned,
remains. He conveyed the fact
that ninety-five per cent
of our imports come by sea
(although he did not qualify
how this was measured) and
said *we should not forget.*
To elaborate his point, he noted:
*Most of our children think
bananas come from a shop.*
So we were entertained with cocktails,
a brass band, and jaunty flags.
There was something of universal
appeal in his argument for the retention
of the ships, the mention of children,
and protection of our bananas.

Laurna Robertson :

KISS

It was done only in public—
at airports, at the foot of gang-ways
when I was leaving or coming home.

No air kissing either, but honest lip to lip,
lip to cheek, plosive contact
and *Safe journey* or *Welcome back*.

My two-dimensional parents
—the background I drew on—
never said that they loved me.

They smiled from the sideboard
in black-and-white battle and wedding dress,
steadily outflanked by school

and graduation photographs. I moved away.
Phoned my messages. *Merry Christmas.
Happy Birthday. See you soon.*

And I miss them. I hug close
my hand-knitted childhood,
my unkissed parents

and their faith in me.

James W. Wood:

THE POOL

It's night. Tearing out of the house,
leaving your clothes where you leave them,
you race more and more naked to where

the moon floats on the surface,
a blob of white in a black garden.
With a yell of triumph you feel

the concrete sliding and let go,
sailing through the fall-freezing air
for a few seconds. Hold it there:

you're poised above something
you know nothing about, about
to dip into the unknown—

but you don't care. With another beat
of the heart it will all be over,
the jig will be up. You splash,

and ripples split the night and all
that's left after a few seconds
is a slight unsteadiness of moonlight

that bounces off the pool as you stand
shivering by the back porch
laughing nervously, drying your hair.

Tom Cleary:

ON BASSENTHWAITE THROUGH BINOCULARS

The grey streaks of scree below the summit
turned purple in close up. On the far side
the fields doubled in the lake as a green smudge.
The sky in the water was a film of milk.
A low hill stared at the sky.
A streak in the water changed from silver
into thirty or so goosanders in single file,
red-brown heads bobbing like apples in a barrel.
Their sawbills curled into a hook,
discreetly closed. They edged forward, pioneers
on their sinewy trek from the known world
of mackerel scales glittering in the sun
towards the dark shadow of the unknown.

Stephanie Green:

A VISITATION

A spraint, a paw-print
in kelp-strewn sand.
These were my only sightings.

I kept watch at Baltasound
for shadows rippling across the road
from salt-water to fresh.

I waited every evening
for the underside of waves
to turn into undulating fur.

On the last day,
when I had stopped searching,
he rose up from the sea.

Slicked with dreadlocks,
he stared me out.

Martin Edwards:

WHALES

Naked as whales,
in our attic of glass

we kicked off the covers
and surfaced among stars.

We were
huge and graceful and slow

precise and tiny
in the southern oceans.

Niall Campbell:

NORTH ATLANTIC DRIFT

We lay together in a run bath
and thought over the rowing boat
that neither one was rowing,

the evening berthed at the bath side
with its vowel song and habit
of staying with us for a while.

The low hall light behind us,
implied only where her breast,
her hip, undressed from the water.

That night the usual swell and drift
delivered my old spoilt thought
of whether a life like this is long

or long remembered—the shirts
receding in the corner shadows
dropped as weights, or anchorage.

Tom Vaughan:

CARTHAGE

Pious Aeneas didn't bother to say goodbye—
he slipped away in silent ships. He said
he often heard strange voices in his head:
it was better to do what they wanted, without asking why.

Dido? Up the stairs to her last bed
where only flames caressed her. While she fried
she turned towards the sail-specked seas, and sighed,
not knowing she'd meet him again in Book Six (when dead).

But he, who grasped the tiller in his hand,
whose sailors grumbled to be once more at sea
whatever he told them about some promised land,

was the hero of an epic—fortunately
for him a genre not concerned to understand
irrelevancies of personality.

Martin Parker:

THE SHARK AND THE VEST

Wear your vest on the beach while you're fishing
or you'll catch the sun, Mum said.
But what I was doing was wishing
that the makers of vests were dead.

None of my friends had mothers
who sent them out in a vest
and I wanted to be like the others—
or better. Or even the best.

And that meant hunting sharks in a pool
without a Chilprufe vest
or be teased for the rest of my time at school
for being so sissily dressed.

So before I started to hunt my shark
in the pool among the rocks
I hid my vest without a qualm
under a stone with my socks.

And I left it there among the rocks—
which turned out for the best
since at night, when the sea reclaimed my shark,
it also took my vest.

Andrew Sclater:

THE SEARCH FOR MY LATE FATHER IN MID-OCEAN

Under a trapdoor in the rough mid-Atlantic
you're outwitting Nemo
on your waterlogged pillow.
Your life in our ozone was, oh, worse than frantic,
now over your body
the sailing ships go.

So down through these cavernous submarine halls
I circle to find you, great spring-boarding father,
splashing your propagules into my eyes,
like an oversexed sea lion—on second thoughts, rather
more of a sperm whale
with a skull full of balls.

Long ago dead, your remains retain light,
dingily tragic
but bright sometimes, magic,
twinkling like trash in the foul sea of night
where I plumb for your body
suspended, pelagic,
capturing rays where you last luminesced—

then think that I glimpse you, though partially blinded,
where you waver with weeds, piscatorially minded,
mistrustful of morse and womanly life-vest,
still swinging your horn-pipe but doing your damnedest
to stick to your guns
and sink both your sons.

Anne Caldwell:

AFTER THE FLOOD

Do you remember the stench of animal hides,
that unholy cramming together,

the racket of snorts,
groans from the lower decks?

Do you recall the creak of the clinker boat,
night after godforsaken night,

the wind in your heart,
my sickness?

That morning, my darling,
clouds were scuttled. You blinked

into the sun's disc, stared at uncharted water,
fresh archipelagos on the horizon.

Forty days and forty nights
had turned your lips papyrus-dry.

Our prow nudged land. Our bodies
were two new coins, minted in light.

M. R. Peacocke :

EASTHAM STREET

Afternoon. The chip shop is closing.
Opening hour now for terrace doors.
Wedges of shadow hold ajar
the terracotta, flaking brown,
ginger and glossy beige.
Hopscotch pavements gleam.

This is the old women's time.
Belayed on cords of fraying breath
they rock on broad shoes to the top of the street
to settle on benches, screaming
like harbour gulls. *Forgot yer pinny, Doris!*
One wears a comfortable hat.

Lightly the northwest wind brooms aside
trash of clouds and words.
Propped on a taffrail of houses,
the old women cruise till tea
on salt unvisited blues and greens
of the distant bay.

J. O. Morgan:

from 'IN CASTING OFF'

*

Some days the fishing smack bobs unladen
for hours, upheld on the tips of the sea's fat fingers.
So he stands out at the prow, makes himself weightless
to the pitches and slams of the water, stares into sea,
his gaze to bore through each thick green wave
as though they are but paper walls behind which
timid fish may be hid; that turning this corner, or this one,
or this, will at length place boat above cowering shoal.
Whereupon he signals the gear to be lowered, and
braces, for the anchor-effect—as the nets fast fill.

*

David Ford:

EVENSONG

At the end of the day
he stands on the bridge
and smokes a cigarette.
Each sunset he relives the day's
raw crimes and calculates his loss.
He watches the city throw its net
of lights upon the river,
haul in its catch of dark.

D. A. Prince:

UNDOING TIME

It was so simple. Slipping the hands
in secret he launched a whole shipwreck
of schemes, just by altering the clocks.

Stealing back twenty minutes took the check
off order, let time, unanchored, drift
on lazier tides, towards uncharted rocks.

Arrangements sanctioned by his shift
of policy foundered on the sands
in bays of submerged seconds: off-course

they were flotsam, their mechanical tick-tock-tick
no longer countered. All at once the force
of time was nothing, just a gentle grip

his frail wrists could dissolve. He'd thought the ship
of life a sober, decent cruise; no slick
to foul its passage, a discipline too pure

to yield to sabotage. But once he'd learned the trick
of slackening the cables, he was sure
he could untie the whole day's careful moorings,
leaving its raft of plans unhitched and insecure.

Kristian Evans :

DEPARTURE

Standing among the rocks
on the sand, your fare in your hand.
Your first trip alone.

Then
nowhere accepts you
all at once.

                And you go.

BY ROAD

Lorna Dowell:

IN CASE

She did not learn to drive or ride a bike.
Would not travel on buses, nor be driven
under bridges, in case hooligans dropped
boulders and bricks from above.

Stuck Elastoplast over a varicose vein
for fear it might rupture. Never had a phone
(germs can be spread by aural contact).
Used an embroidered handkerchief

to cover her mouth when she had to
use the public call box, that once,
to talk to a doctor.
Never mentioned the smell of urine.

Buried her husband's ashes
in a casket in a suitcase. Kept
plastic flowers beside his crash helmet
and sausage-finger gloves

like objets d'art on the sideboard
by the front door, as if waiting for him
to pick up and leave. Would not go away
because dust would build up in her absence.

Patricia Ace :

BULL

When I drive up the glen to my daughter's school
I pass the white bull standing stock still
at the fence, his muddy arse green as guano
or that dark molasses that passes from babies
sometimes as they are born, a sign of distress.
The bull looks too bored for distress—
his low-slung head, a ring through his nose—

but the thing that draws my eye each time I pass
is the pale orange scrotum,
the huge bollocks hanging down,
like a sack of sweet potatoes, skin stretched
to a thread by the weight of them ...
the gravitational pull of all that unlived life, life, life
teeming inside.

Janet Loverseed:

JE M'ENNUIE

My sister Liz, the boring little fart,
was always one for word play. Mum would ask
Who'd like a drink of Vimto? and she'd say
Now what's its anagram? Vomit, remember?
And one dinner time our brother Tom said
I feel like a chocolate pudding and she said
You look like a chocolate pudding
and he bashed her.

And once in London in a taxi, she said
Traffle Gar on purpose for Trafalgar.
Tom said, *Shut up, the driver'll think
we're country pumpkins.* I sighed, *Je m'ennuie*
to sound posh, but Liz just chortled, *That means
you bore yourself. Why'd you do that? We're having
a ball on Paul Maul.* Mum shouted *Big 'eds!*
Then she bashed us.

Lydia Fulleylove :

NIGHT DRIVE

So when the phone call came, saying
that we should go back tonight, we were barely
surprised, we might have been waiting
for it all our lives. We took two cars in case
it did not happen that night and one of us
at least could drive home to sleep and I
followed my father so as not to lose my way
through the twisting lanes in the dark
but I think it was marked in my head
and I would not have faltered even
though all the time I was thinking
of my mother, the bones stretching
her beautiful skin and her left eye almost
closed, her face as clear as the rear lights
of my father's car or the sign of the inn
where we'd eaten that morning.
There was nothing to do but keep on
driving, the car flowing between the banks
until at last we were crossing the glare
of the town to the place where my mother
lay dying, though perhaps not tonight,
we knew that the end might not be tonight.

Matthew Stewart:

DAD ON THE M25 AFTER MIDNIGHT

Even before the front door's shut
he's in first gear—up past Tesco,
third exit from the roundabout
and onto the slip road at last.

This is where the housework and kids
recede, junction after junction.
He could head west, then north, then east
—with just a millimetric nudge

of the wheel—but he holds a lane,
perfecting this nightly circle.
It closes back in on his name.

Sue Butler:

HUNGER

When you call round, demanding
the last of your things, I make tea,
tip chocolates from a bag
into your cupped hand. They spill
until you hold just one—
a heart. We stare at
the awful power of chance. And I know
I'll never smell chocolate again
without thinking of this. Us. Bravely,
I pick it up, careful
not to touch your palm. I let it melt
on my tongue. Eat another,
another—even the spilled ones.

Outside in sleet your dark hair
is plastered to your head
as you load your car—books, socks, ties.
Two shirts escape, ghosts
in a fight. One flies down the lane.
One waves.

Gill Andrews:

TOM POTTER

A man on the bus smiles at me and I stumble because
for a millisecond he's Tom Potter, a man
who held dice in the bowl of his hand and
never revealed when he'd use them.
Tom Potter was enormous as the Bank of England.
I'd phone Tom Potter and he'd say Sorry but do nothing.
I'd visit Tom Potter, he'd sparkle and call me
Darling, do nothing. The man on the bus looks down,
embarrassed. I too look down, embarrassed.
I will always be the woman who once knew Tom Potter.

Theresa Muñoz:

PERFORMANCE REVIEW

now
walking fast
away

hands in pockets
fresh air

who cares who cares who cares

but I do

I get on the bus

poor concentration
work ethic
we must reassess

her hard look
as she says this

I thump my fist
against the glass

forget it forget it let it go

the bus bumps along
turns a corner

but I don't

Alison Prince:

EARLY BUS

Headlights breast the hill,
too far off for any sound
except the tide's wash
slapping the sea wall.

The indicator winks,
engine chuntering,
windows steamed up,
a fug of talk inside
like a travelling pub.
Up two steps, pass ready.

Harbour, love?

    Yes, please.

Doors have hissed shut.
The insect bus
creeps on towards Brodick, while outside
dawn tears the black sky open
like a tangerine.

Lois Williams:

FORMATION

Clocks back, the Novice walked with us
from catechism to the bus stop.
Dusk at four, exodus of children
over farmland to the main road.

Once, late, the bus already gone,
an hour to waste—the luck of it—
she showed us Doddson's sheep
flocked in the paddock.

Their faces turned to us,
testing us, smelling the incense
steeped into our coats,
the human tinge beneath it,

and they moved as one large animal
into the field's deep middle,
letting us cross without letting us close,
teaching us the untaught geometries.

Margaret Christie :

MODULATION

Anton Webern says
This is modulation:
Go out of your flat, to go for a walk,
And go on a tram, then a train, then a ship
To another continent. But modulation works
When you know your way back to the home key.

The key to my home bent
The night I ran out to a rehearsal
Without the music, ran back to the flat
When I realised, and still got the bus.

I had another key,
Modulated smoothly
From F to B sharp:
Temperament restored.

C. J. Driver:

ILLEGAL IMMIGRANTS

Walking on the hillside behind Stanley
We found them—five young men, all dressed oddly
And frightened. We thought they must be students
Till they begged for food, using sign-language.
The children ran to the car without asking
And brought back oranges and biscuits, all
That was left of the picnic. The hungriest
(Or the least frightened) gestured at the sun
To show its movements and then held up four
Thin fingers to show days without eating.
He also gestured us to telephone,
Wrote the number down on an old packet
And, as we left, held his hands to his heart
Like a dancer, to show us he loved us
Or whoever answered would love him too.
In the car, I crumpled up the packet.
No one asked any question. I noticed
Our eldest, the tough one, the ruffian,
Hid his face carefully at the window.
I want this poem to be plain and simple.

Marion Tracy:

from 'GIANT IN THE DOORWAY'

mother's back in front of me in the car
is straight like a wall and her neck is tall
she's holding herself up with correct posture

her hair smells and is made into golden sausages
she unpacks our things in the cornish holiday cottage
lennie puts two dinky toy trucks a red racing car

mother's face is smooth only her eyes aren't right
and a fire engine onto the window ledge
look how close to the sea!

Kate Scott:

SOME AFTERNOONS

Some afternoons I take her out in the car.
We go fast. Fast, with the windows down,
the wind winding its fingers round
our hair, its palms pressed hard
against our cheeks.
I drive to feel the brief unfastening
from this life of close-knit tasks.
She laughs at the wind, at the slant of sun
playing on her face. This is a run,
dreaming of driving to the edge, and then beyond.
I can see the rooms where we would stay:
camel-humped beds and crumbling wallpaper;
the glass of wine in the bar; me suddenly sexy
in another language, wearing her like an accessory,
light as a bracelet. For this is about weight,
the weight of a life, the daub and mottle of walls
that last, and when running you shed things,
like a snake with his snake-hide behind him.
I begin to brake without thinking;
the pull is acceleration in reverse.
We are meshed in the home walls,
this small child and I,
the hair and earth of its frame.
We are balancing on a world
that keeps turning,
however fast we run.

Michael Munro:

TRAJECTORIES, MULL

Out of the van
a break to stretch the legs,
a respite from cassettes and cigarettes.

Down to the water,
my scuffed cowboy boots
skittering over sea-polished shingle

discovering my cold fingers yet apt
for the boy's art
of skipping stones.

Out of the body's memory
the hand's shape, stance,
and sculpted launch

to send the flat stones skiting,
smacking through the soft waves,
fast and loose.

Wait a moment more,
then back to the narrow way west
and the road's end—Iona.

Martin Reed:

RIGHT TURN

The last snow clings to quarry-scars and hedgerows:
Clee Hill, couched ten miles away. The cool air
makes him see how, river-like, this road flows
into it, how all the land's hunched strength knots there.

He leaves its course here every day to thread
the frosted lanes. The morning light just suits
rough corrugations of the hill's rucked bed
to his desire for risking other routes.

The Clee humps after him behind each hedge
and he can almost hear its ancient mirth
of waters working in a dry stone wedge.
This mesh of roads can't bind the restless earth.

He drops to second gear to take a bend.
The radio unfolds a woman's voice
whose soothing music has the power to mend
and almost make his journey seem like choice.

Cliff Forshaw:

ROAD KILL

What is this stuff with tails? This slump of fur
that mimes the body's weight, intimates
the slow tug of earth that gets us all. You swerve
to miss these weird speed bumps, glimpse
a forested ridge in the marginalia of the road,
a premonition of mountains in that spine's hump.

Each is a map to what still lies, lies still
—yet moves—now like a wave, now flat-out:
roadstone's quake, asphalt fever, that tremor
shivering towards you through the heat-haze,
visions of angels skating on the shimmer.

Blind bend. Horn. The dopplered blare
through ears and car and ribs. Road train.
Chained logs, knee-trembled, hovering on compressed air.

Charlotte Gann:

COLLECTED

Her shift over, she shimmies out of nylon skin, pricks
her finger hard on the badge-pin. Snaps shut
her locker door, like one life closing. The other waits

purring in shadows, slinking forward along the kerb.
She emerges from a narrow side street, slides
into his passenger seat without a word. As they pass

the infirmary, the cigarette factory, the museum
of Egyptian mummy heads in yellow bandaging, she leaves
each one in flames. He opens up on the motorway.

The sea is rising, black, choppy. Gone, the picture
postcard. 'Remember *The French Lieutenant's
Woman*?' he asks. She remembers only *The Collector*.

Rosie Miles:

WHEN I AM DEAD, MY DEAREST

remember I lived under the Aston Expressway
in a room of concrete girders and crisp boxes
held together with twine. Tell the cars
how I foraged and fumbled for a life worth living
among the abandoned mattresses and drunken trolleys.

Bury me here, in the rubble, forty foot under
the exact point where the IKEA and DFS lorries pass
and tell everyone you know who never knew me
how much I loved this place: the city's dirty underbelly,
the inescapable hum.

Stephen Payne:

JOURNEY HOME

On every long journey home, there's such a place.
It can be just a roundabout or a slip-road,
perhaps a farmhouse gable, a stand of trees.

Always the same small shift as it's passed,
the journey in some way over before its end.

In company, the conversation changes pace.
Alone, the mind gives itself away,
clicking into calm, or else unease.

BY HORSE

Michael Mackmin:

THE KISS

A kiss. The kiss. Just lips touch, press,
she kissed him, stepped back, looked,
he looked too, she turned, calm,
went out to where her husband sat
on his horse, stuck her hat
on her head, swung up, rode off
the two of them together, leaving.

He drove home 'O she kissed me' joy
sweat his skin fizzing 'Why, she
kissed me.' She told him 'We're going,
leaving the country, south, for good.'
Kissed him, dared him, 'If you want me,
stop me.' The horse hooves thud
in the pine forest. He let her go
but kept the kiss, fed on it
long after it was fresh.

Graham Austin:

AFTERTHOUGHT

The stable door is bolted now.
The trouble is, of course,
that that is just exactly how
we can describe the horse.

Ruth Marden:

LITTLE JOCKEY

Bronze figure, Hellenistic period, National Museum, Athens

Absurdly small for your horse,
urchin or sprite,
did you suddenly drop from a tree,
slip neatly astride his spine?

Where are the others?
Your face flicks sideways to check.
Lips thrusting, you shout,
keyed for a final spurt.

Never still,
you seem not to ride so much as contrive
a flight through air.
Your every muscle swells
and the charge carries through to your toes.
Spread elbows crook,
knuckles grip
on phantom reins.

I've never wanted anyone
so much to win.

Maria Taylor:

THE HORSE

Everyone says I should get back on the horse.
I sneak up on her, but she's too quick,
she rams her hooves into my hoof-proof vest.
Too bad, horse. I may not be able to get back on you
but I know the score. I'm used to getting back on horses.

*

The horse is grazing in a field.
I have prepared complex equations
for getting back on horses. I nod at the farmer
who's seen others trying to saddle up.

*

It's early evening and meadow sweet.
There's a kind of light that drives poets crazy.
I pad over softly to my horse,
now at rest in her stable. I sing to her
with such tenderness even a judge would sigh.

> *My love, my light, oh meadow sweet mare*
> *may I could I . . .*

She smiles a gentle smile of buttercup teeth.

*

Morning. Drizzle. Horse laughs.
I am a joke on many social networks.

*

Horse is my editor. Horse is Dustin Hoffman
in 'All the President's Men'. *You wanna get back on me*
you're gonna have to do it my way, say her conker-coloured eyes.

She pours strong coffee, rests her hooves on the table.

※

> Sweet horse, gentle horse
> let me know your warmth—a touch
> of your mane.

Darling horse, I wrote you a haiku.

※

> As horses go I have had my fill of horses. There's nothing special about you. You're just like all the other horses and let's face it you're no looker. See I snapped my pencil in two. Go neigh at the moon, Equestriana.

※

Horse is strapped to my desk,
her snorts are pure anger.

> *Say that again, horse, didn't understand.*
> My partner appears at the door, aghast.
> No *worries, private joke*, I say.

※

It's on a Thursday I mount her.
I was out for bread and milk in town,
she was trotting along beside me. So humble.
She even buckled her knees to make it easier.

> Thank you, horse.

> Bless your stirrups and your saddle.
> Let me stay on.

Jon Stone:

THE NEW DOCTOR WHO

He was sighted in London, 'a great tall blacke man'.
A party of ten were sent out to bring him in,
among them Slaughterford and Jenny Greenteeth.

In Framlingham, word of his wickedness spread.
Three sisters confessed to assisting him.
Learned tracts were published on the Continent.

In April, he passed through Haughley, high
on a police horse. Braziers spat cinder-mouthfuls,
lit the kindling of dawn. A wind bowed.

Poor Black Shuck never came back from the mist.
Balladeers' voices guttered in their throats.
I wrote to John: *A traitor lives among us.*

The Sabbat was held as usual, though many
had hidden or taken the form of rocks
and even the wine had a steely aftertaste.

Some say he wears finely tailored suits
and will sit down to think, chew on livestock.
He laughs when I tell him this. His mouth

is a forge and his laugh is ironmongery.
'How long did you say you were staying?'
'Well now. I don't think I did.'

Chrissy Williams:

ROBOT UNICORN ATTACK
A love poem for a video game

Possibility bursts like a horse
full of light, accelerating
into a star. Explosion. Hit
< x > to make your dreams
crash into stone. Death.
Diatonic chimes of joy.
I want to be with you.
Let dolphins fly in time.
Swim through air, leap
past sense, past sin and then
hit < z > to chase your dreams
again. *Always. Harmony.* Up,
smash goes the rainbow-trailing
heart again. Again. Again, again!
I want to be with you when
make-believe is possible.
I want to be with you when
robot unicorns never cry, hit
stars collapse in quiet love.
When there is only love.
Harmony. No shame.

Richard Osmond :

IF MY INSTRUCTIONS HAVE BEEN CARRIED OUT

the King of Norway
will be pictured on horseback
hunting wild boar
in the margins of this page.

Frank Wood:

WORDS TO EAT

When you were about two
and in your pram,
and I'll never forget it,
the tripe and trotter man came round
with his horse and cart
shouting *Tripe!* as he went
along the street. And you,
and I'll never forget it,
joined in, shouting
Chipe! Chipe! Chipe!
I can still see that man's face.
He wasn't at all pleased.
And whenever we had prunes for tea
you used to say, *Don't want
any those dirty pums.*
You always called them 'dirty pums'.

Well, I've gone through life
avoiding dirty pums,
except during the war
which I'll never forget,
and shouting *Chipe! Chipe! Chipe!*
which hasn't pleased some people,
and if I ever do forget
and start eating dirty pums
and swallowing chipe,
it'll be because I'm too far gone
to tell the difference.

Helen Tookey:

PRAIRIE

Sometimes we are girls, and sometimes horses.

When we're horses, we can gallop, but there aren't so many stories.

When we're girls, we wear calico dresses and never any shoes.

Calico is always striped, like sticks of rock, and crackles when we run.

Sometimes we live in the dug-out, and sometimes in the new house.

The new house is made of shiny yellow wood, and has real glass windows that really open.

The new house is square, like a doll's house, and sits exactly flat on the ground.

The new house smells of yellow wood, and all the rooms are clean and empty, bright boxes of yellow air.

There are no other houses anywhere, only prairie.

The dug-out is dark and cool and makes us feel like hunters.

The dug-out smells of earth and is full of the sound of water, the creek running just below.

We lie flat on our bellies and watch the water-creatures, and we are something like the water-creatures, or like otters perhaps, thin and

brown and sharp-eyed, slipping silently into the water,
speaking the urgent language of hunters.

This is the unrolling of *prairie*.

Prairie is the widest word we know.

Jim Carruth :

RIDER AT THE CROSSING

A preacher told me these moments are in every journey:
slow weeks of no relief from saddle sores and damp
where the cogs of old age stretch your bones on a rack
and your last winter coughs its way through spring.

Hunger never leaves but squats in an empty stomach,
halted by a day when the neigh and nose of your horse
seem lost forever somewhere in the fog.
Up ahead, the rutted track gives up the ghost

and the worn hooves of your one companion touch
the start of water—she lets you know by a splash,
a shiver in her spine. You dismount by an old ferry bell,
pull on its ragged tail, its tongue pleading for response,

railing against a silence that saps the river's voice.
Away from there, strangers travel other roads
but you're stuck in this moment, no longer moving,
staring into an absence, straining for the faintest sound—

a clue to the other side, some shape forming or lifting—
when all that's left to wait for is a change in the light.

Alison Brackenbury :

LAMINITIS

Sick at heart, not as sick as the pony
hobbling on her hind feet, I lead her in.
Rich grass seethes in her blood. She cannot be
at ease, shifts, flexes fetlocks, stares at me.

Here's the bucket with the drug stirred white.
Will she always be lame? No time to think.
Let her lick all; say (as a parent might)
Give it twenty minutes. You'll be all right.

Kick down the crumbled shavings of her bed,
a softer chill beneath her burning feet.
Brush off her scurf and dust. The watch-hands speed.
Her fidgeting grows slow. She drops her head

and chews, as horses do, relaxed, at peace,
sinks down her quarters, sags each glossy knee,
stretches (white with wood dust) her back legs straight.
Weightless, half-closed, her eye stays fixed on me.

Jo Field:

WATERLOO

One foot in the stirrup, the other
in the mud, he says:
We shall have sharp work today.
Saddle-leather clamped between his thighs
he spurs the hours forward.

Another horse is shot from under him,
another found. Again and again
they come, led skittering on their toes
or planting their heels
to brace themselves in elegant *levades*.

Battle blunts senses with its particular hot stench,
its mangle of sound and colour,
the blues and greys and red as far as sunset
and the final charge of Vivian's hussars
to triumphant rout.

Later, on a table in the town,
he remarks the instruments perhaps
are not as sharp as they could be,
but through it all his heart pumps
quite unaltered. When the leg at last

is separated from his body
only his eyes betray him, watching.
As a new mother might watch that part
of her which is her dead child
borne away.

ON FOOT

Deborah Trayhurn:

BEFORE WE COULD FLY, BEFORE

Before we could fly, before
ride in a car, coach or train
or be carried along on
a wheeled frame, or on the back
of any tame animal
and before the knack of barques,
I would not have met you—though
if continents had yet to

split, feet would have carried us
perhaps a little further—

otherwise I would be here
and you there with no thought of
each other but a yearning:
that across a haunted space,
beyond reach, like a planet
or moon still unfound, only
waiting for a lift, is you.

Ross Kightly :

LANDSCAPES

Some people on certain days will tackle
wind dust rock sand Gila Monster deserts

short blue-green freezing afternoons
on the pack-ice wrestling polar bears

even slime-green dank dark crab-scuttling
coastal caverns close to high tide

in search of skull-guarded
pirate treasure-chests

they'll balance across razor-edged ridges of
mountain ranges barefoot in shorts and t-shirt

and on some (few) future days
I might go too if you would come

but I think today tomorrow and
the next day and the day after that

I'd prefer to take the walk past the nice houses
at the Square and the swallow barn

through the gate not over it this time
and up the rocky slope laughing

past the gorse lair of the Woolly Wolf
to the wind-torn lone hawthorn

with or without the sudden curlew
that might or might not flash across

to the easy sheep slope down to
the coast the mere and the castle.

We know we can do this any day
and it will never ever fail us.

Matt Merritt:

CURE

Wait for one of those wide open October days.
Wake early to hear the house stretch its aching frame.
Feel the heat start to sing through its veins.
Fall asleep again

until the light is sharp enough to trim
the frayed edges from your life.
Grab breakfast while you bag them up—last night's terrors,
everything broken or bent out of shape.
Be careful though. Best use good strong sacks
because they will try to escape.
Stash them, struggling, in the back,
then drive to somewhere that is only earth and sea and sky,
with a wind so big that your tongue catches in your throat
and your head, your whole body is clean and free and light.
Empty them out.
Bosses from hell, bad hair days, back pain, bills.
Hangovers, hang-ups, hours of headlights
smeared on grimy gridlocked streets.
Chances gone begging. Disappointments. Defeats.
And words—unkind or unspoken or unheard.
Let them go.

Feel better already? Good.
Return home at your own pace.
Relax. Walk into winter unaided.
Remember to keep the sacks somewhere safe.

Frances Corkey Thompson:

THE OLD WOMAN WISHES FOR A ROAD

Make me a road I can walk once more—
a road with white houses, on a white shore

and there must be sand, banked well
and scattered, ground out of shell

out of bone, out of stone in the sea's eye—
a road under rain, and a wind to dry.

Then I'll hitch up my skirts and I'll run, shouting—
I'll run with the children, shouting, shouting.

Jeremy Page:

SNOW

At dead of night
I fly into a city
made silent by snow.

You wait for me
in the house by the canal,
a bean with a heart
beating inside you

and in the days
that follow, we walk
and walk, snow
on our boots,

take buses, trains
and trams, and never know
the moment when
that heart stops beating.

Weeks later
in another snowbound city,
we begin to discover
what we've lost.

At dead of night
your grief is yours,
mine mine.

Ruth Pitter :

THE LOST TRIBE

How long, how long must I regret?
I never found my people yet;
I go about but cannot find
The blood-relations of the mind.

Through my little sphere I range,
And though I wither do not change,
Must not change a jot, lest they
Should not know me on my way.

Sometimes I think when I am dead
They will come about my bed,
For my people well do know
When to come and when to go.

I know not why I am alone,
Nor where my wandering tribe is gone
But be they few, or be they far,
Would I were where my people are!

Annie Fisher:

SACK RACE

Sports Day morning; a quick run-through.
I herded them out to the field.
Forty-two in the class that year.
Didn't bother with actual sacks—no time for that
but I showed them what to do, thought
I'd made things clear

till the race began and I saw her jumping
half way down the track—
big bouncing hops like a kangaroo,
just the way I'd taught them to.
But she'd got it all wrong. *What on earth
is she doing?* She had the sack over her *head.*

Has she forgotten that hot afternoon?
The scratch and smell of a hessian sack,
speckled sunlight through rough rope-weave,
surging voices, burning breath, the unseen crowd,
and a skinny, brown-limbed girl
(must be a woman now)
all alone and leaping in the dark.

Kate Hendry:

MY FATHER CARRIES HIS DEATH TO ME

I thought I was dying, he says, *dying.*
I said to J on the night of the party
'I'm not going to make it till the end.'

I turn from the washing up
to hear him. He's making coffee
on the other side of the kitchen.

Adrienne Rich carried her death
in her pocket like a raincoat.
Mine is with me at the table

like the shells I've brought in,
wet and glowing from the beach,
though their colours fade inside.

His death is with him like the small
white stones he lines up by his front door
to help him find his way home in the dark.

Tom Duddy:

SMALL TOWNS

Driving on certain summer days
into small, dark, lightly littered towns
(the ones without a café or police station

where the public houses are shut
as grimly as little prisons until
sometime towards evening),

you may pass a woman striding, arms folded,
along the dry-blue road out of the town,
looking for all the world as if

she is breaking the spell
of the long, desultory days,
and loosening all holds upon her.

Gill McEvoy:

FIELD OF BUTTERCUPS

A whole field oiled by sunshine;
we scamp through it like children,
laughing as we part the yellow ocean
wave on wave, exclaiming at the million
gleaming faces lifted to the day.

No need to hold them underneath our chins:
we're wading home with butter on our feet.

Andrew Philip:

MAN WITH A DOVE ON HIS HEAD

The man next door has a dove on his head.
He can't remember how it got there,
but those who've seen the evidence suspect
it hatched amongst his springy curls.
We don't know where he goes each Wednesday,
but he returns cooing to the bird and streets.
Although he's used to stares, the giggles,
taunts and nicknames scunner him. We ask
about support groups, fellow sufferers
and those who've come through the condition.
He says, *This dove is here for the duration,*
and tells us *There are far more than you realise*
who wander round with a bird on their heads—
a dove, a parrot, magpie, rook or hawk.

Kirsten Irving:

NANCY ARCHER STEPS OUT

Dr. Isaac Cushing: She will tear up the whole town
                                            until she finds Harry.
Deputy Charlie: And then she'll tear up Harry.
        —Attack of the 50-Foot Woman, 1958

Dreading my period. It'll be more of a plague
than ever. But more than this
I dread putting my bubblecar eye
to the window of the club where I know you sit

in love, or joined by something stickier than the floor.
Honey and honey, I want my shot
but if I take my thumb and dash your heads
into the Bacharach-piping jukebox
or stake you with a huge incisor
and write LIARS in your combined juices,
it will be a half-cough of revenge, the kind
that doesn't quite clear the throat.

That's not to say I won't.
The moon's a thumbnail. Guess
I'll sit on the bar stool of the cooling tower
until I work out
what to do with myself.

Patrick Yarker:

SHOES

My father sets his great black shoes by mine
on the mat of newsprint. He's snaked each lace
through with a snap and thumbed the little propeller
to open the tin. A puck of wax
whose shine the bristles steal. Listen! They whisk
sudden as gusts of rain across his shoes.

Into the scuffed toes of my daughters' shoes,
along the flanks, around each stiff scooped heel,
my cloth-wrapped fingers work the buttery wax.
Colour of moleskin, smell of turpentine.
Their shoes wait beside my shoes on the mat
absorbing night, and in the morning shine.

Peter Jarvis :

TAKKIES

Takkies kicking balls in parks
Takkies sockless with khaki shorts
Takkies worn with skirts and doeks
Takkies crammed into rackety combis
Takkies pushing pedals on bikes
Takkies queueing at factory gates
Takkies toyi-toying at anxious cops
Takkies laceless on drunken skollies
Takkies jiving to the kwela
Takkies dangling out of bakkies
Takkies soaked with muddy stains
Takkies whacking schoolkids' bums

This is where you'll always find them,
takkies, takkies, Bata's takkies,
in boxes stacked up to the rafters
at Shoprite, PEP and Bailey's,
in every dusty country store

and stencilled on the sides of the boxes:
BE SMARTER, WEAR BATA

David Kinloch:

CAIN'S WIFE

I was a tiller, a sower, a hoer, a sewer,
a siever, a scyther, a shearer, a reaper,
a planter, a mower, a herder, a milker,
a minder, a plougher, a thresher, a gleaner;
with no time for a name of my own.

Then he killed Abel and I was
a drifter, a tramper, a marcher, a prowler,
a runner, a walker, a hiker, a rover,
a ranger, a jogger, a beggar, a hawker;
with no time for a name of my own.

There was desert and wold,
bush and veld, steppe and silt,
mould and dust. I was gravel.
I was pebble. I was flint, I was turf.
And I dreamed of a space

crossed by voices that raised me,
by arms that held me
and hands that offered me
to lips that kissed me
with no need for a name or a time.

Alan Hill:

from 'GERONTION'

*

My friends and I sit
like elderly passengers
waiting for our planes.
When a flight is called, someone
rises quietly, and leaves.

*

Walking down Hill Street
I passed by the premises
of *Prostate Scotland*—
a chill reminder. Would it
had been in some other street.

*

I fart as I walk.
Forget tolerance, wisdom,
insight, peace of mind.
The reality of age
is this: you fart as you walk.

*

Groaning helps. Stiffened
upper lips impress, suggest
classical learning,
though don't abate pain. But yes,
groaning definitely helps.

Lydia Kennaway :

WALKING FOR WATER

Walking for water is not
going for a breath of fresh air,
a pilgrimage,
a stroll,
a hike.
It is not
a parade,
a protest march,
a sponsored whatever.
It is not a way
to stretch your legs,
or have that conversation.
Walking for water is not
to see an unmissable sight.
It is not on anybody's bucket list.

It is the flight of a migrating bird,
a cruel calculation of distance, fuel
and energy burned.

BY AIR

Paula Jennings:

SWAN

from 'The Change: Woman as Several Kinds of Bird'

She's learning to run again
on the surface of the water.
Her black webs beat a flight path
and the great swags of wings
hold tension with such poise
that her hollow bones fill with light.
She's remembering how the whole sky opens
to the white spear of her neck,
how the evening loch rushes to meet her.

Hamish Whyte:

FIRST AND LAST SWAN

First swan I remember
was a match.

This one, patrolling
the same short stretch
of river is alone.
I can't tell whether
cob or pen, suspect
it's been widowed.

It has space to fly away
but chooses to stay.

It preens, it pokes
at the sedge,
sometimes chummed by one
or two ducks.
The heron paid
a visit but kept
its distance.

You want to save it
but from what?
Is it not a swan's job
just to be, to be there,
light against the dark?

Tim Love:

IRON BIRDS

You lay out words to tempt them,
another poem about poetry.

Rhyme radio valves with light bulbs.
Rewrite airstrips with painted decoys.

Ancestors can't save you. Burn your foodstores.
Murder the medicine men. Empty your shelves.

You have seen them flying overhead.
They will come again. You will write about

how their vapour trails are like the broadening,
fading scratches on your lover's back.

Gerry Cambridge :

THE QUEEN

There's something almost vulnerably human in the way
The wasp, below the wine glass I've inverted
To a clear cell on my kitchen sill,
In pauses between her quartering, combs
Out each long antennae with a foreleg—
First one, and then the other,
Like a girl teasing out her tats,
Holding the fankled strands between
A forefinger and thumb;
And suddenly back to waspishness
With blurring spasms of wings,
Antennae quiverings—
Scaling her cliff of glass on pricking feet.

I only want to briefly look at her.
She is a queen, newly awake from her winter sleep;
In the flex and pulse of her abdomen are stored
Ten thousand summer wasps, wasp dynasties
Down the perpetual light of centuries;
And she will be adored.
But, for now, she rests, her segmented antennae
Drooping and her jaws, so secateurish,
Slightly open, as she clings against her prison glass
With the disconsolate air of a scunnered spaniel
Gazing out, not even angling her plated face
When my gigantic head
Looms like an instant mountain into view.

It is Easter Sunday; she wants to begin
Her own fierce story of resurrection
Though they would kill her still,
Those bleak gusts of March
And that high, wasp-heedless blue.

Fiona Moore:

NIGHT LETTER

I don't believe in an afterlife
any more than you did
but sometimes at night I lie awake
and can't not imagine you
floating, out there
somewhere between angel and ectoplasm,
because sometimes this is easier
not only for the heart
but for the mind too.

It feels almost disloyal
to you, who said again
there was nothing
after we'd been given the prognosis:
said it calmly, factually. So
if you're out there, please
forgive me for imagining
you, out there.

Helen Evans:

TODAY'S TASK

Mark the maps. Let today be the day
when the aircraft fits you like your favourite coat
and the winch cable clunks into the belly-hook
with a sense of belonging

when you release into six knots up
and a few turns take you so high
that the place you were standing ten minutes ago
might as well be a model airfield

when long lines of satpic lenticulars
visible overhead now
invite you to cross sea and mountains
to your out-and-return's only waypoint:

a set of co-ordinates chosen by you
where no other glider has been.

Alan Buckley:

GRAVITY

The aerialist swings out, hair rippling,
beyond the proscenium arch. Just below
the dead point, where upward force
and downward pull are perfectly matched,
she lets go—we gasp—of the *corde volante*,
and there, for a heartbeat, body and rope
are floating apart. Later, she'll smile:
*Whatever you choose to think, I cannot fly. I fall
professionally.* But the woman above us now
is not the one with tied-back hair, calloused
hands, who carefully checks the shackles
and silks before the audience comes. She
has vanished, as we all have, briefly released
from our fragile, desperate weight.

D. A. Prince:

BLACKBIRD

He's landed on his feet, this one,
blinking in criss-cross frenzy of ants
fired up on hot stones. They run
zigzag, anyhow, freestyle; black slants
of panic, pepper-dust, while he's claw-deep
in tea-time, picking them off,
ripe as berries. He's hopping, squaring up,
landing new angles, straight in, trough-
eager, happy as Puck.
Just out of the nest, and can hardly believe his luck.

Will Harris:

MOTHER'S COUNTRY
(Jakarta, 2009)

The shutters open for landing,
I see the pandan-leafed
interior expanding
towards the edge of a relieved
horizon. Down along
the wet banks of the Ciliwung
are slums I have forgotten,
the river like a loosely
sutured wound. As we begin
our descent into the black
smog of an emerging
power, I make out the tin
shacks, the stalls selling juices,
the red-tiled colonial
barracks, the new mall …
It is raining profusely.
After years of her urging
me to go, me holding back,
I have no more excuses.

Gina Wilson:

AVIAN

We know our angels by their plumage
and flight, taking off with a running jump
like mallards, or like swans
climbing out of deep lakes on thunderous wings

crick-necked, crook-shouldered as a heron
shaking out bony folds, cranking up his gear
or blue as the kingfisher's lit fuse
scorching the air, then not there

buzzards outstretched circling Gower
or red kites over Oxford, scaling the heights
on our wedding-day, seeming to say
No limits now, no limits!

My own particular, arriving at the back door
like a robin, head on one side, watching,
waiting for the penny to drop, departing
with the clean flick of a wren.

Clare Best:

AIRMAN

Flying Officer Ray Bédard, aged 25, was flying from RAF North Luffenham in a Canadair Sabre MK2 on 23 June, 1953. He broke from formation and was killed after bailing out while his aircraft was in a steep dive. The plane crashed in a field by Whitehouse Farm near Boston in Lincolnshire.

There's still the geometry
of lanes and dykes and hedges,
a spirit-level horizon. East, the North Sea
sheet-metal smooth to the sun.
West, a thousand fields beyond Long Tankins

hundreds of nameless shades of green.
Now, as then, the invisible skylark
rehearses, rehearses. The marsh harrier
glides low over wheat, drops on a vole.
Hares lie in hollows, unblinking.

Robin Vaughan-Williams:

THE MANAGER & I

We are getting on just fine.
He has taken me under his wing.
If I pull at the feathers
I find maggots wriggling just beneath.
But he doesn't mind.
He is magnanimous in his way.

Sometimes we fly in a V-formation
with his other protégés
over warehouse and distribution centres
ringed by wire fences, held together
by a network of mini-roundabouts
and the red ribbons of empty cycle lanes.
These places would be hard to reach on foot.
Flying is much better, he tells me.
We hold hands and for a moment I feel safe.

Then the skin slips from his palm and I find myself
clutching at a hollow glove.
I wave at the people down below as they race to greet me.

Martin Cook:

FALLING

After Chagall's 'Les Fiancés de la Tour Eiffel'

We should never have climbed that phallus.
We were, after all, Brits and when you heard
a squeaky fiddle playing Greensleeves
and thought you saw your pet goat taking off
from the Eiffel Tower towards Spain,
you went goofy and leant out to stop it.

I over-balanced trying to save you
but landed, with you in my arms
on a big duck with a cock's comb.

You'd forgotten your goat and were
clutching a blue fan and dreaming of cherubs
while I had the Kama Sutra on my mind.

Neither grotesque birds nor angels
with violins and silly wings could save us;
we wasted an expensive wedding gown.

Sally Festing:

SATURDAY MORNING

He's drifting. Look! 8.30 Birds

> She watches the thatcher,
> cap and white, flourish his yelmer,
> sprout wings and levitate—a harvest angel
> stabbed against pine trees in morning sun.

He's flying over our house. Where will he land?

> She sees the hands, small and vigorous,
> pull straw, pat, smooth with headrake,
> working to T-shaped pins. So finicky, it seems
> she has never looked properly before.

Can you see the man?

It's Saturday. They shouldn't be in bed with
books and breakfast and binoculars. He wonders
about her marginally different view.
Fumbling, she refocusses.

Are you watching the balloon?

Hanging basket, burner-flares skim on air.
                Birds chorus.

> She sees the glitter of speckled gold,
> a halo and two quick hands.

David Hale:

DEADMAN POINT

    adrift up here
        unstitched by sea and sky
I feel stoned on ozone
    kite-like
        buffeted by the breeze

    in need of wire or weight,
        something to hold down
this canvas self
    that's soaring on a thermal
        fuelled by distance

    by perspective
        by the white under-spray
of waves broken
    on black rocks,
        far below

Diana Gittins:

from 'BORK!'

Maisie has returned from the wilderness
of broodiness
abandoned her virtual nest, her eyes
no longer wild,
her chest no more on fire.

She shakes her gawky frame,
preens her messy feathers, looks

around in shocked surprise

as when a passion—soul-consuming,
mind-regressing, heart-obsessing—
lifts
and drifts away, leaving
feet and flesh
earthbound in the everyday.

Geoff Lander:

THE DIABETES LEGACY

Sir Frederick Grant Banting, KBE MC FRS FRSC, 1891-1941

Should you visit Musgrave Harbour
where Atlantic breakers roar

by that battered—nay macabre—
piece of debris from a war

in Canada (its eastern coast
adored by kittiwakes)

do say a prayer and raise a toast
for diabetics' sakes.

The gruesome wreck was partly due
to Goebbels' fascist ranting.

War was why the bomber flew—
alas for Frederick Banting.

Bound for tests on syncope
with Wilbur Rounding Franks[1]

Banting died beside the sea
amid the twisted cranks.

---

1 Wilbur Rounding Franks helped develop the G-suit to combat pilot black-out (syncope).

Reflect there on his early death[2]
and life-long discipline,

on bravery[3], his final breath
and the role of insulin[4]

and read the plaque, lest you forget
the youngest ever laureate.

---

[2] The scientist survived the plane crash but died the following day of exposure and his injuries.

[3] Banting had won the military cross at Cambrai in 1918.

[4] In 1923 Banting and John James Rickard Macleod received the Nobel Prize in Medicine. Banting shared the prize money with his colleague, Dr Charles Best. At the time of writing, Banting, at 32, remains medicine's youngest Nobel laureate.

Helen Nicholson:

SOFTENING

The day you died, we'd a soft
argument about guillemot wings.
You won. I like to think I let you.

I never saw a guillemot, nor
its wings. Nor was there a 'you'
or a 'we' in such proximity.

But, my dear, it is such a comfort
to imagine us, our shy wings
untied—us, unstoppable,
bickering about lanolin.

BY RAIL

Rob A. Mackenzie:

GIRL PLAYING SUDOKU ON THE 7.14

I sit down opposite. She doesn't blink
or cough, her pencil-scratch the only noise
beyond the train's dull chitchat. Teenage boys
slouch up the centre-aisle, unleash the stink
of Lynx. She keeps on scrawling to the brink
of suffocation. I admire her poise,
open windows, plumb my brain for ploys
to start a conversation. I can't think.

Our eyes squint out of sync. Although I stare,
I don't dare interrupt her concentration
and when she finally completes the square
I focus on the floor. One hesitation
begins a chain. I set up solitaire.
The train heaves on, already past my station.

Olive Dehn:

ON A CLEAR NIGHT

This train rolls up to Ulster,
This hoarse determined train;
This moon sails back to London
To spy through every pane.

Oh why must I rush northwards,
Why must this thing befall?
Whilst she sails back to London
Who loves you not at all.

If I had power to snatch her
From where she flies so fleet,
I'd pull her down and bind her
In this drab corner-seat;

I'd snuff her silly brilliance
With hat and cloak and glove,
And sail away to London
And lie beside my love.

Gregory Leadbetter:

PERSEPHONE ON THE UNDERGROUND

She was already half way there.
In the funnel-web of London,
between platforms
under the layers of Waterloo,
she heard her train plunge out of hiding around a corner.

She started to run, and as she ran
sprigs of dried heather fell from her
with the grace reserved
for the darker seasons.
You would have thought she was made of a whole garden

as she crumbled into the oncoming air—
into rosemary, sage and poppy-heads,
apple-mint and thyme—
a ticker-tape of rose-petals
celebrating her stumble.

Marilyn Ricci:

THIS IS A PASSING TRAIN THAT WILL NOT STOP

nevertheless I get on
head down to the buffet
a beer maybe two as
we shoot up country
speed past wildlife
the slippery can cool
hook my finger in the
loop crack and psst of our
secret my eyes chase horses
through a spree of green as we
pick up pace making tracks
don't need a map to go back
to the buffet for a couple of
shorts or four unable to pull
the communication cord
brake at signals fly by
stations lurch down the aisles
through the tunnel of love to
meet Johnny Walker rattling over points burning
bridges makes no odds this train won't stop
it will not stop stop stop stop stop stop stop

Charlotte Gann:

CORNERS

Once he's done she makes him up a nice bed
for the night. Takes sheets and blankets, neatly
folded, from the linen cupboard outside
her bedroom and carries them down the stairs.
While he enjoys a final cigarette
and scotch in the small walled garden, she smoothes
the sheets out on the put-you-up mattress,
then tucks them tight in hospital corners.
Early next morning she cooks him breakfast:
tea, orange juice with bits in, soft boiled egg,
two slices of white toast and marmalade,
sweet black filter coffee boiled on the hob.
She walks him to the station, allowing
plenty of time for him to buy a bar
of chocolate and a newspaper, and still
be comfortably on the 9:23.
It's only after his late train pulls out,
and a passing friend, concerned, touches her
back gently, that she bends double on
the pavement outside the station, and cries out.

Christina Dunhill:

LOST

Perhaps they lost their art, their heart,
their soul, their shoes, a library card.
Perhaps they lost a coat, a cap,

a mobile phone, a map. Perhaps
the teeth on the main zip slipped—
there was no grip, there was a gap.

Perhaps they lost their wits, their which,
their way, their finger on the homing key,
their who, their why, their ticket to today.

Vishvāntarā:

TO PLATFORMS

I hope you read this; if you do
you'll see how I remember you
though seasons may fly past with scarce
three thoughts applied to your affairs.

Twelve years since our October glance:
my coward soul escaped its chance.
Whatever hour slipped off that edge
calls after me along the bridge.

Eleanor Livingstone:

RESTORE POINT

No, wait.
Turn back the hands
on the station clock.
Five misspent minutes. Catch
the pigeon in mid air
his wings spread
like a cut-out. Throw
that bag of crisps
back up onto its loop
and free the coins
that paid for it.
Relieve that woman
of her rucksack;
drop it gently
to the floor. There.
Freeze our words
at that point

and send us out
onto the empty
platform, carrying
our conversation
lightly with us
into the cold night air.

Even two minutes
would do, the rucksack

neither up nor down
the pigeon almost
on the beam
his feathers straining,
the bag of crisps
falling, the change
fallen, our sentence
broken, the train
still standing
on platform three.

Stephen Payne:

IMP OF THE PERVERSE

Heels on the yellow line, you eye the track.
Of course it won't happen, although the tug
feels ineluctable. You don't step back
but shrink deeper inside your coat, part shrug,
part flinch. A small step for a body, *ergo*
it comes to mind. All you can do is make
some promises, hug last night's warmth, and argue
your way through. Suppose free will is fake.
Darwinian selection couldn't tend—
surely?—toward a trigger-happy brain
which, loaded with your experience, would end
things just because it sees how. Then again,
what kind of brain is mustering this doubt?
In a moment, the train will find it out.

Alan Buckley :

THE ALCHEMIST

The four-year-old boy knows the joy of it,
though he doesn't understand how it happens,
as he runs, snugged up in a duffle coat
on the sandstone ridge between
the windmill and the observatory,
pretending to be one of those trains—
woofing a trail of clouds behind it—
that's recently vanished from his world.
He sees his breath hang in winter's brightness.

He never gets bored of this casual alchemy,
the unseen made visible, something outside him
taken into his body, changed, and then
let go; a swirl of mist that's him
and not him intermingled. Though this
isn't what the boy's thinking. He's remembering
a big black engine, its warm oil smell,
as I am now. We stand wide-eyed,
each printing his ghost on the generous air.

Marcia Menter:

STRANGERS ON A TRAIN

He wasn't you, but he might as well have been
because he was the image of you, this stranger,
and because even now you are strange to me.
He was all briskness and angularity
like you—eager as a dog to please
on the surface, wary as a cat within.

He took the seat in front of mine on the train,
clearly a traveler, not a commuter like me.
A man helped lift his case to the luggage rack
and I looked up and saw in a sort of slow-motion shock
that he was not you, but you as I'd seen you last,
madly preoccupied, chewing gum too fast.

Tall and long-boned with a scruffy beard
and restless eyes—you to the life,
though younger—with your dancing energy
and that careful smile of one who has been hit hard.
He thanked the man in a tenor voice like yours
and touched his arm in that gesture, warm and rehearsed

you used on me. Yes, I loved you more
unreasoningly than I ever loved anyone,
and the love was real; but it might as well have been
directed at this man in the navy suit
(you would have worn a much more casual shirt)
now sitting in front of me, jiggling his left foot.

I stared at the back of the stranger's neck—which bore,
unlike yours, curly hairs and a red birth mark—
and silently said the prayer I so often said
for you, but meaning every word for him:
May you be free from pain and free from fear;
May you know how worthy of love you are.

He seemed to become less restless in his seat
though I could, of course, have been imagining that.

Maria Taylor:

TRAVELLING ON THE 10:21 WITH TOM HARDY

Hardy calls to his dead wife
at Castle Boterel, St. Andrew's Tower.
He calls quietly over Wi-Fi,
Can it be you I hear?

Fields fly without answers.
A smudge of rabbit hops away
and vanishes into a grassy tuft.
A horse's silhouette awaits a rider.

My heart's a dog-eared *Metro*.
I hold my book under the table
as if I'm keeping his love a secret.
I am. We're both out of style

amid a one-upmanship of screens.
His simple question skims the roofs
of expanding towns. It pauses
over a clock's stopped hands.

Paul Stephenson:

DISPOSAL

10, 20, 40 minutes ... and so the delay grows.
A voice appeals to the hordes of travellers
scattered beneath the departures board:

'Mesdames, Messieurs, would you please
stand well back as the bomb disposal unit
proceeds to blow up a suspicious package.'
(She uses *détoner*. Latin gave us detonate.)

We take in the bang. Await the all-clear.
Look up for a platform, run for the train,
pull out, pick up speed, miss connections.

Colder in Belgium. Light flakes are falling.
Brel is singing to me—

Il est brisé, le cri
des heures et des oiseaux,
des enfants à cerceaux
et du noir et du gris.

It is broken, the cry
of hours and birds,
of kids with hoops at play,
broken, the black; broken, the grey.

Il neige sur Liège
and the river has nothing to say.

Jennifer Copley:

LEEDS CITY STATION, 1918

I'm coming home, he'd said.
See you, Friday. Under the clock.
She waited all day and the next,
scouring the platforms, even venturing
into the Men Only bar.

For twenty years she sat in the same place
where she could see the trains.
The station staff got to know her
and provided tea. She liked it strong.
Sometimes she spilled the sugar
so she could write his name in it.

The nicotine from her cigarettes
stained the wall in the shape
of his face and wide shoulders.
His eyes were so blue they could stop night falling,
she told the waitress as she cleared.

Ramona Herdman:

HE PRETENDS HE DOESN'T KNOW THE WAY TO THE STATION

Gorgeous. Inappropriate. He keeps stride
till I work the talk around to my boyfriend,
then he peels away like a shark, wishing me
every happiness. I check my pockets
all the way home—I can't work out
what I'm missing. Until I realise that this
is another of my escape poems.

I still see him cruising the shoals of commuters,
silver-beautiful as a trick of the light.
I never looked at him full on. It reminds me
of those stories where you go under the hill
with the King of the Faeries and dance
till everyone's dead. Back and forth
on the 7.40, the 17.02.

D. A. Prince :

THE SUNDAY NIGHT PIANO

Rolling in on the late train, halfway
between the weekend's open autumn fields
and Monday's ring-fenced desk, hearing
tired wheels rub the shine off the concourse,
dodging a sober pigeon checking crumbs,
the final Eurostar emptied, *lattes* gone stale,
you catch a first tangle of notes.

A cleaner halts, balanced
on the handle of a long day's mopping-up,
and listens. Blue iron arches
hold back the darkness, poised
over the phrasing. Is it Schubert?

He's left a *Lidl* bag slumped by his feet,
this man, last of the many players of the day,
bringing to life the loneliness
laid in the keys, his lover's touch
knowing by heart what's hidden. One by one
the shops put out their lights. The cleaner stirs
and shuffles with his mop. The steps
turning away to join the Northern Line
have never seemed so hard.

Peter Gilmour:

OLD MAN

This fumbling on the threshold for his key
is new. It is not drink or depression,
he assures me. Sometimes he drops the key
and can hardly pick it up. Shadows come,
born as of pain, as he struggles there:
you can see them claiming him, one by one.

Especially when he gets the key to work—
pure chance, like whether he will see next spring—
he laughs at himself, his laugh like an arc
over gravely darkening continents,
and turns towards the street to wave and smile
for always there is someone there, watching.

I see him now as though on a platform
across from mine, looking through the windows
of a passing train, from light to dark,
frame by frame, until the train has gone by
and the following silence returns him—
older than he had ever planned to be—
to solitude, symptomatic trembling
on the threshold, that business with the key.

Jim C. Wilson:

MR MACCAIG CAME TO STIRLING

Central Library, January 1991

I was the would-be entrepreneur; he,
without doubt, the star. Unfolding, he smoked
below my big *No Smoking* sign. Then,
dragging a leg, he faced his crowd. A joke

as dry as finest malt, then Mr MacCaig
was away, off through a world of short walks
that ended with long conclusions; then sheep
and stone; mortality; and trains. He talked

to us a complete hour, with measured words,
quick gleams and perfect pauses. In his streets
and hills, we saw with his eyes, knew Scotland
and eternity. He even stood to treat

us all with Hints About His Writing.
How long did he take to make a poem?
He answered well, but didn't tell. Some folk
called him *Norman*, as though they were at home

with an uncle or old pal. And the stags
stood quiet by the birch wood, while the white horse
bared its teeth at the wind. Later, I sped
through the night with Mr MacCaig. The view

from the train was ourselves: me, and his long head
smoking and talking, through Larbert, Falkirk,
Linlithgow. Until he started to sing
to me, as though he'd known me forever—

but Norman could sing for almost anyone.
The train rolled on; it slid into our station.
Shutters were shut; the clock's hands close to midnight;
but frosted pavements shone like constellations.

Mark Halliday:

NOON FREIGHT

That's a long freight chackling along
over there behind the Acme Market
while you eat your turkey melt
where you are in your life, in Wilmington Delaware.
This freight train: unmistakable metaphor—
those boxcars of many shades (many if you look closely
though at first glance mostly drab)
loaded with stuff, stuff gathered from the past
intended for the future, rolling faster than you think
compelled by a force out of sight far ahead,

long rolling metaphor: freight train.

You've seen how many, probably four thousand freight trains
and at least fifty of them looked meaningful;
life is so prodigal with its metaphors
as if patronizing us, as if to give us every chance
to grasp something awfully basic, some big point

rackajack a rackajack a rackajack a rackajack
it's a long freight train, metaphor
so rhythmic you never quite grab the iron handles
and hoist yourself on board

this long freight train, you feel it will never end
on those embanked tracks up behind the Acme Market
never end, those boxcars of many shades and

such worldly pragmatic insignia,
then you look down at your sandwich
                               in Wilmington Delaware
and the freight train
           is gone

tracks empty as if nothing had passed
and that's another

and you feel a silence in the wake of metaphor
and then it's nice (but small) (but nice) that your turkey melt
is still there and you can take it literally.

Peter Daniels:

MR LUCZINSKI TAKES A TRAM

He has paid a small coin to a glass box
like a fairground machine.

A dull purple ticket
permits him to sway with the tram

which pushes on through a city of breezeblocks
and neo-baroque stucco.

The people might be
his second cousins twice removed:

a woman in fishmonger's gloves
coming home from the market,

a man balancing two dusty old bikes
between fellow-passengers.

In this incarnation, his tweed suit
is not quite threadbare enough.

He hasn't lost his sense of direction but
it has nowhere to take him.

Somewhere at the end of this line
is a field of dandelions and a bluebell wood.

Gerry Cambridge:

FROM A STOPPED TRAIN NEAR ARBROATH

Astonishing me now is how
those horizon clouds, magnificent and calm,

such miles away,
framed by the carriage window,

are also with us here—
the original space travellers.

That girl could see them if she looked,
miniature cumuli

beamed across the world
and built again by photons with minute precision

on every attentive
or uninterested eye.

Helena Nelson:

WARNING

The train may be longer than the platform.
The platform may be shorter than the train.
The poem may be longer than your patience.
This one stops here.

ACKNOWLEDGEMENTS

All poems in this anthology have previously appeared in previous Happen*Stance* publications or, in the case of Alison Prince, in a collection jointly published with Mariscat Press.

Patricia Ace, 'Bull' from *First Blood*, 2006
Gill Andrews, 'Tom Potter', from *The Thief*, 2010
Graham Austin: 'Afterthought', from *Fuelling Speculation*, 2010
Clare Best: 'Airman', from *Treasure Ground*, 2009
Alison Brackenbury, from *Shadow*, 2009
Alan Buckley, from *The Long Haul*, 2016
Robbie Burton, from *Someone Else's Street*, 2017
Sue Butler: 'Hunger', from *Arson*, 2011
Anne Caldwell: 'After the Flood', from *Slug Language*, 2008
Gerry Cambridge: 'The Queen', from *Notes For Lighting a Fire*, 2012 and 'From a Stopped Train Near Arbroath' from *The Annals & Other Poems*, 2019
Niall Campbell: 'North Atlantic Drift', from *After the Creel Fleet*, 2012
Jim Carruth: 'Rider at the Crossing', from *Rider at the Crossing*, 2012
Margaret Christie: 'Modulation', from *The Oboist's Bedside Book*, 2007
Helen Clare: 'Gerris Lacustris', from *Entomology*, 2014
Tom Cleary: 'Goosanders on Bassenthwaite Through Binoculars', from *The Third Miss Keane*, 2014
Martin Cook: 'Falling', from *Mackerel Wrappers*, 2007
Rose Cook: 'Casting Off', from *everyday festival*, 2009
Jennifer Copley: 'Leeds City Station, 1918', from *Some Couples*, 2017
Peter Daniels: 'Mr Luczinski Takes a Tram', from *Mr Luczinski Makes a Move*, 2011.
Olive Dehn: 'On a Clear Night', from *Out Of My Mind*, 2006
Lorna Dowell: 'In Case', from *Crossing the Ellipsis*, 2011
C.J. Driver: 'Illegal Immigrants', from *Citizen of Elsewhere*, 2013
Tom Duddy: 'Small Towns', from *The Years*, 2014
Christina Dunhill: 'Lost', from *Blackbirds*, 2012
Martin Edwards: 'Whales', from *Rainstorm with Goldfish*, 2012
Helen Evans: 'Today's Task', from *Only By Flying*, 2015
Kristian Evans: 'Departure', from *Unleaving*, 2015
Sally Festing: 'Saturday Morning', from *Salaams*, 2009
Jo Field: 'Waterloo', from *The Anglesey Leg*, 2015
Annie Fisher: 'Sack Race', from *Infinite In All Perfections*, 2016
David Ford: 'Evensong', from *Punch*, 2010
Cliff Forshaw: 'Road Kill', from *Tiger*, 2011
Lydia Fulleylove: 'Night Drive', from *Notes on Sea and Land*, 2011
Charlotte Gann: 'Collected' & 'Corners', from *Noir*, 2016
Peter Gilmour: 'Old Man', from *Taking Account*, 2011

Diana Gittins: extract from Bork!, 2013
Stephanie Green: 'A Visitation', from Flout, 2015
David Hale: 'Deadman Point', from *The Last Walking Stick Factory*, 2011
Mark Halliday:'Noon Freight', from *No Panic Here*, 2009
Will Harris: 'Mother's Country', from *All This Is Implied*, 2017
Rosemary Hector: 'Bananas', from *Knowing Grapes*, 2014
Kate Hendry: 'My Father Carries His Death To Me', from *The Lost Original*, 2016
Ramona Herdman: 'He Pretends He Doesn't Know The Way To The Station', from *Bottle*, 2017
Alan Hill: from *Gerontion*, 2016
Kirsten Irving: 'Nancy Archer Steps Out', from *What To Do*, 2011
Peter Jarvis: 'Takkies', from *Nights of a Shining Moon*, 2015
Paula Jennings: 'Swan', from *Out Of The Body of the Green Girl*, 2008
Ross Kightly: 'Landscapes', from *Gnome Balcony*, 2011
David Kinloch: 'Cain's Wife', from *Some Women*, 2014
Geoff Lander: 'The Diabetes Legacy', from *The Lesser Mortal*, 2018
Gregory Leadbetter: 'Persephone on the Underground', from *The Body in the Well*, 2007
Eleanor Livingstone: 'Restore Point', from *The Last King of Fife*, 2005
Tim Love: 'Iron Birds', from *Moving Parts*, 2010
Michael Loveday: 'Desert Island', from *He Says / She Says*, 2011
Janet Loverseed: 'Je m'ennuie', from *The Unripe Banana*, 2007
Rob A. Mackenzie: 'Girl Playing Sudoku on the 7:14', from *The Clown of Natural Sorrow*, 2005
Michael Mackmin: 'The Kiss', from *Twenty-Three Poems*, 2006 (also in *And*, 2007).
Ruth Marden: 'The Little Jockey', from *The Little Jockey*, 2014
Richie McCaffery: 'Dedication', from *Spinning Plates*, 2012
Gill McEvoy: 'Field of Buttercups', from *Uncertain Days*, 2007
Marcia Menter: "Strangers on a Train', from *The Longing Machine*, 2007
Matt Merritt: 'Cure', from *Making the Most of the Light*, 2005
Rosie Miles: 'When I am dead, my dearest', from *Cuts*, 2015
Fiona Moore: 'Night Letter', from *Night Letter*, 2015 (also in *The Distal Point*, 2018)
J.O. Morgan: extract from *In Casting Off*, 2015
Theresa Muñoz: 'Performance Review', from *Close*, 2012
Michael Munro: 'Trajectories, Mull', from *Poems for Alice*, 2007
Helena Nelson: 'Warning', from Unsuitable Poems, 2005, & in *Down With Poetry*, 2016
Helen Nicholson: 'Softening', from *Briar Mouth*, 2018
Richard Osmond: 'If my instructions have been carried out', from *Shill*, 2014
Jeremy Page: 'Snow', from *In and Out of the Dark Wood*, 2010
Martin Parker: 'The Shark and the Vest', from *No Longer Bjored*, 2010
Stephen Payne: 'Imp of the Perverse', and 'Journey Home', from *Pattern Beyond Chance*, 2015
M. R. Peacocke: 'Eastham Street', from *Honeycomb*, 2018
Andrew Philip: 'Man with a Dove on his Head', from *Tonguefire*, 2005
Ruth Pitter: 'The Lost Tribe', from *Ruth Pitter, Selected Poems*, 2010
Alison Prince: 'Early Bus', from *Waking At Five Happens Again*, 2016
D. A. Prince: 'Blackbird' and 'Undoing Time' from *Nearly the Happy Hour*, 2008;
 'The Sunday Night Piano', from *Common Ground*, 2014

Martin Reed: 'Right Turn', from *The Two-Coat Man*, 2008
Marilyn Ricci: 'This is a Passing Train that Will Not Stop', from *Rebuilding a Number 39*, 2008
Laurna Robertson: 'Kiss', from *Praise Song*, 2014
Andrew Sclater: 'The Search for My Late Father in Mid-Ocean' from *Dinner at the Blaws-Baxters'*, 2016
Kate Scott: 'Some Afternoons', from *Escaping the Cage*, 2010
Paul Stephenson: 'Disposal', from *The Days that Followed Paris*, 2016
Matthew Stewart: 'Dad on the M25 After Midnight', from *Inventing Truth*, 2011
Jon Stone: 'The New Doctor Who', from *Scarecrows*, 2010
Maria Taylor: 'The Horse', & 'Travelling on the 10:21 with Tom Hardy', from *Instructions for Making Me*, 2016.
Frances Corkey Thompson: 'The Old Woman Wishes for a Road', from *The Long Acre*, 2008
Helen Tookey: 'Prairie', from *In the Glasshouse*, 2016
Marion Tracy: extract from title poem of *Giant in the Doorway*, 2012
Deborah Trayhurn: 'Before we could fly, before', from *Embracing Water*, 2009
Robin Vaughan-Williams: 'The Manager & I', from *The Manager*, 2010
Tom Vaughan: 'Carthage', from *Envoi*, 2013
Vishvāntarā: 'To Platforms', from *Cursive*, 2015
Hamish Whyte: 'First and Last Swan', from *Hannah, Are You Listening?*, 2013
Chrissy Williams: 'Robot Unicorn Attack', from *Flying into the Bear*, 2013
Lois Williams: 'Formation', from *Like Other Animals*, 2017
Gina Wilson: 'Avian', from *Scissors, Paper, Stone*, 2010
Jim C. Wilson: 'Mr MacCaig Came to Stirling', from *Will I Ever Get to Minsk?*, 2012
Frank Wood: 'Words to Eat', from *Racing the Stable Clock*, 2012
James Wood: 'The Pool', from *The Theory of Everything*, 2006
Patrick Yarker: 'Shoes', from *Patrick Yarker: A Sampler*, 2010

About HappenStance Press

HappenStance Press was founded by Helena Nelson in May 2005. Since then, over 150 publications have materialised—most of them poetry books of various shapes and sizes. The press is independently funded, a not-for-profit enterprise, proud of its poets and its lively subscriber base. No fewer than 103 Happen-Stance poets feature in this anthology. They're a friendly bunch, excellent company on any journey.